MASTERS OF MATHS

Captain X

here to rescue you from Times Table Trouble

Buster Books

First published in Great Britain in 2005 by Buster Books, an imprint of Michael O'Mara Books Limited, 9 Lion Yard, Tremadoc Road, London SW4 7NQ

A CIP catalogue record for this book is available from the British Library.

ISBN 1-904613-92-6

10 9 8 7 6 5 4 3 2 1

Visit our website at www.mombooks.com/busterbooks

Printed and bound by Bookmarque Ltd, UK

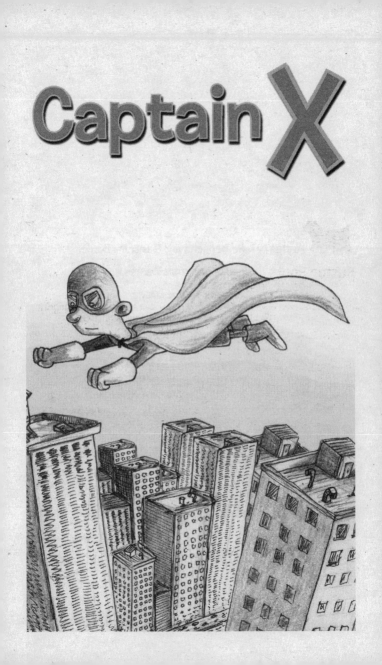

Written by Luke Bennetts and Samantha Barnes

Edited by Samantha Barnes

Designed by Zoe Quayle

Interior illustrations by Niki Catlow and Zoe Quayle

Cover illustration by Martin Chatterton

Contents

Captain X

Captain X, the Masked Multiplier, needs your help to deliver the world from maths mayhem. His arch-enemy, the Complicator, is causing chaos with his crooked and villainous deeds.

Can you save the day?

The city is in a state of confusion; time has been scrambled, robbery is rife, and a strange spell has left people in a daze. Do you have the maths genius to stop the Complicator and foil his wicked plans?

Keep your wits about you at all times. The Complicator has set up a network of tricky number traps, riddles and games to keep you and Captain X busy.

The future of the world depends on your super skills. Use Captain X's ingenious shortcuts and tricks to tackle the times tables and outwit the number villain.

The Missions

By the time you reach page 82
of this book you will be fully
trained as a master of
multiplication and ready
to embark on a series
of missions to defeat
our villain.

Your first mission appears
on page 84.

The missions will test every
skill that you have learned.
DO NOT attempt them until
you are fully trained or
you may fall foul
of the Complicator!

All the skills you need
to complete the missions
are in this book. You may
need to go back through the
book to remind yourself how
to tackle a sum.

If all else fails, the
answers to all the missions
are at the back of the book.

Multiplication Mayhem

The Complicator likes to use multiplication sums because they can easily be made to look difficult. But you're not so easily fooled!

As Captain X's new super sidekick you can solve these sticky sums and save the day.

Let's look at a way to simplify multiplication sums. Perhaps they are not as complicated as the Complicator would have you believe...

Multiplication as Adding

Multiplication is really just a quick way of adding numbers together.

Look at the following sum:

$$2 + 2 + 2 = 6$$

In this sum you are adding 2 together 3 times. A quicker way to set out this sum is by using multiplication, like this:

$$2 \times 3 = 6$$

Imagine that Captain X takes a break from saving the world and decides to go shopping for some new superhero underpants. His favourite underpants come in packs of 4. He buys 3 packs.

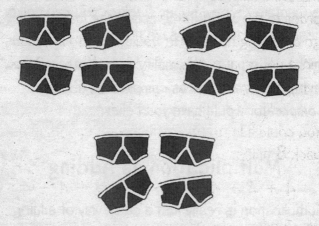

By counting up all the underpants you can see that Captain X buys 12 in total.

You can also work out this total by adding the 4 underpants in each pack 3 times:

4 + 4 + 4 = 12

This is the same as doing the multiplication sum:

4 x 3 = 12

It is simple to use addition with a small sum like this. But when numbers get bigger the process becomes very boring.

Imagine that Captain X (with your help) defeats the evil Complicator and returns mathematical order to the world. To celebrate, he may decide to go on a long holiday. He would need to buy loads more underpants. What if he buys 8 packs? How many underpants would he have now?

You could add together the 4 underpants in each pack 8 times:

$$4 + 4 + 4 + 4 + 4 + 4 + 4 + 4$$

Which equals 32 underpants. But this takes a long time, and it's not much fun sifting through so many underpants, even if they do belong to a superhero!

A quicker (and less embarrassing) way to do this sum would be to use multiplication:

$$4 \times 8 = 32$$

The Complicator would try to make you add all the numbers together, simply because it takes longer and looks more complicated (which is, of course, what he likes best). But now you know what to expect from our baddie, you can foil him with your multiplication know-how.

Putting Multiplication Sums in Order

Multiplication sums can be done in any order.

You can count Captain X's **4** underpants per pack **8** times:

$$4 \times 8 = 32$$

or count **8** packs each containing **4** underpants:

$$8 \times 4 = 32$$

and the answer to the sum is the same.

This is true of any multiplication sum.

Times-Table Talk

Captain X's arch-enemy, the Complicator, has a list of different and confusing ways to ask maths questions. The language of multiplication can seem tricky. But it isn't. Just be prepared for the ways in which sums might be disguised.

For instance, 4 x 8 could be written as:

4 times 8
4 lots of 8
4 multiplied by 8
The product of 4 and 8
Multiply 4 by 8

The Tables

The times-table grid below is a secret weapon.
With it you can find answers to any multiplication
sum from 1 x 1 through to 12 x 12.

Say, for example, you wanted to multiply 8 x 5.
First, find 8 in the column of numbers on the far
left-hand side of the grid (a column runs down

1	2	3	4	5	6	7	8	9	10	11	12
2	4	6	8	10	12	14	16	18	20	22	24
3	6	9	12	15	18	21	24	27	30	33	36
4	8	12	16	20	24	28	32	36	40	44	48
5	10	15	20	25	30	35	40	45	50	55	60
6	12	18	24	30	36	42	48	54	60	66	72
7	14	21	28	35	42	49	56	63	70	77	84
8	16	24	32	40	48	56	64	72	80	88	96
9	18	27	36	45	54	63	72	81	90	99	108
10	20	30	40	50	60	70	80	90	100	110	120
11	22	33	44	55	66	77	88	99	110	121	132
12	24	36	48	60	72	84	96	108	120	132	144

the grid, from top to bottom). Then find 5 in the row that appears along the top of the grid (a row runs across the grid, from left to right).

Move one finger from left to right, along the row in which 8 appears and move another finger down the column in which 5 appears. The answer to the sum appears in the square at which your fingers meet (40).

Now try selecting 5 from the far left-hand column and 8 from the top row and find the answer. You will find the same answer.
That is because:

$$8 \times 5 = 40 \text{ and } 5 \times 8 = 40$$

The answers to all multiplication sums appear twice in the grid, because all multiplication sums can be reversed but the answer stays the same.

Can you find the answers to the following sums, and mark both places they appear in the grid?

$$9 \times 4$$
$$3 \times 7$$
$$8 \times 2$$

Super Squares

A SQUARE number is the result of multiplying a number by itself. For example, 49 is a square number as it is the result of multiplying 7 by 7.

Can you find the number 49 on the times-table grid on page 14?

A Square Route

The Complicator has placed a times-table grid on the ground. Every grid square, except those that contain square numbers, is booby-trapped and set to explode if it is stepped on. Captain X must get across the grid to pursue the Complicator, but can he do it by stepping on square numbers only?

Help Captain X by using the times-table grid on page 14 to mark his route. He can move forwards, backwards or diagonally.
The route is simpler than you might think.
(Answer on page 85.)

Multiples

The MULTIPLES of a number are the answers to all the multiplication sums involving that number. For example:

$$3 \times 8 = 24$$

So, 24 is a multiple of 3 and also of 8.

$$7 \times 6 = 42$$

So, 42 is a multiple of 7 and also of 6.

If you write the multiples of a number in order, you get the MULTIPLICATION SERIES of that number. The first numbers in the multiplication series of the number 3 are:

3	6	9	12	15	18	21	24

and so on.

On the times-table grid on page 14, each row contains the multiples of the number that appears at the beginning of the row, and each column contains the multiples of the number that appears at the top of the column.

The 100-Square

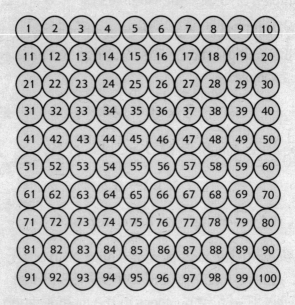

The square above contains the numbers
1 to 100. Starting with 4 and then 6, put a red
dot in every second circle until you reach 100.
These numbers are multiples of 2.

Put a blue dot in every third circle, starting with
6 and then 9. These numbers are multiples of 3.

Put different coloured dots in each circle where
the number is a multiple of 4, 5, 6, 7, 8 and 9.

You will see that the multiples of 6 and 9 are also multiples of 3, and the multiples of 4, 6 and 8 are also multiples of 2. As every number is a multiple of 1, colour in the circle containing 1 as well.

Mystery Numbers

And what about the 25 numbers in the 100-square with no coloured dots in them?

These mystery numbers are known as PRIME numbers. They are not multiples of any number other than 1 and themselves.

This means that the only multiplication sum you can write to equal a prime number is 1 x that prime number. For example:

$$1 \times 17 = 17$$

The first 25 prime numbers are:

2, 3, 5, 7, 11, 13, 17, 19, 23, 29,
31, 37, 41, 43, 47, 53, 59, 61, 67,
71, 73, 79, 83, 89, 97.

2 is the only EVEN prime number.

The Relationship Between x and ÷

Beware, the Complicator may try to destroy you with dirty division. But do not fear! Dividing is just the opposite of multiplying.

Once you know your times tables, you can turn small division sums into multiplication. Look at the following sum:

$$20 ÷ 5$$

All you need to do is find the number that when multiplied by 5 is equal to 20.

$$? \times 5 = 20$$

20 is the fourth number in the multiplication series of 5, as you can see below:

5	10	15	20	25	30	35	40

That is because:

$$4 \times 5$$
$$= 20$$

This means that:

$$20 \div 5 = 4$$

and also:

$$20 \div 4 = 5$$

Putting Division Sums in Order

Unlike multiplication, the order of numbers in a division sum is important. For example, this sum:

$$20 \div 5$$

asks you to find the number that when multiplied by 5 is equal to 20 ($? \times 5 = 20$).

If you reverse the order of the numbers, like this:

$$5 \div 20$$

the sum now asks you to find the number that when multiplied by 20 is equal to 5 ($? \times 20 = 5$). At this point division becomes so diabolical that we'll just have to hope there's a Master of Maths who can tackle this in another book!

Division Disaster

That no-good scoundrel, the Complicator, is causing chaos with his powerful multiplication laser that multiplies anything it hits. Captain X must save the day with his Divider and restore order to the city.

Complete Captain X's division sums
and return the city to its normal state.
(Answers on page 85.)

9 traffic lights **÷ ? = 3** traffic lights

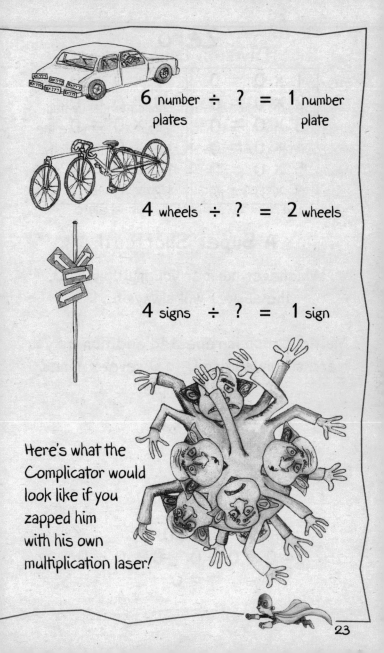

6 number plates ÷ ? = 1 number plate

4 wheels ÷ ? = 2 wheels

4 signs ÷ ? = 1 sign

Here's what the Complicator would look like if you zapped him with his own multiplication laser!

Zero

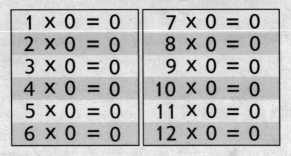

1 X 0 = 0	7 X 0 = 0
2 X 0 = 0	8 X 0 = 0
3 X 0 = 0	9 X 0 = 0
4 X 0 = 0	10 X 0 = 0
5 X 0 = 0	11 X 0 = 0
6 X 0 = 0	12 X 0 = 0

A Super Shortcut!

Whichever number you multiply by 0,
the answer will always be 0.

Multiplication is repeated addition, so you
are simply adding 0 to 0 several times.
For example:

$$2 \times 0$$
$$= 0 + 0$$
$$= 0$$

and

$$6 \times 0$$
$$= 0 + 0 + 0 + 0 + 0 + 0$$
$$= 0$$

The Complicator has heard that Captain X now has a super sidekick - you! He telephones you from a meeting with his band of nasty crooks to warn you not to challenge him.

'So, you are Captain X's latest helper, eh? Well, I have defeated many before you and you cannot compete with my gang of evil henchman. You will quake in your little superhero boots when you hear that I have 100×0 crooks in my gang, ready to do anything I say!' threatens the Complicator.

Why should you not be too worried?

(Answer on page 86.)

One

1 × 1 = 1	7 × 1 = 7
2 × 1 = 2	8 × 1 = 8
3 × 1 = 3	9 × 1 = 9
4 × 1 = 4	10 × 1 = 10
5 × 1 = 5	11 × 1 = 11
6 × 1 = 6	12 × 1 = 12

A Super Shortcut!

When a number is multiplied by 1,
the number does not change.
For example:

$$4 \times 1$$
$$= 1 + 1 + 1 + 1$$
$$= 4$$

and

$$7 \times 1$$
$$= 1 + 1 + 1 + 1 + 1 + 1 + 1$$
$$= 7$$

You follow the Complicator down a dark street where he hands a note to some shifty-looking crooks. Once they have read it, they drop it on the floor and run off.

The note contains the address of a house where the Complicator has hidden some bags of stolen money. Solve the sum on the note to work out the house-number of the address where the money has been stored.

The Complicator has used brackets in this sum as he is using two operations (x and +) in the same sum. The sums in brackets need to be completed first.

(Answer on page 86.)

$$(1 \times 1) + (4 \times 1) + (1 \times 6)$$
$$+ (9 \times 1) + (1 \times 12)$$

Holdup Lane
Badville

The bags of money are under the floorboards in the hallway.
Bring them all to me by midday...or else!
C

Mission 11

The sheriff of Cowboy City
calls to tell you that the
Complicator is up to some
serious mischief.
He wants you to go to the city
immediately. You can either
fly there or drive.

To fly directly to the city is
a distance of 14 miles by air.
You fly 2 miles every 3 minutes.

If you drive the X-Mobile,
you have to drive down
2 main roads which are each
3 miles long, and then drive
down 6 small roads which
are each 1 mile long.
You drive 4 miles every
5 minutes.

What is the quickest
time you can
be at Cowboy City?

Reverse the order of the
numbers in the answer,
and go to this page number
for your next mission.

Answer on page 94.

Two

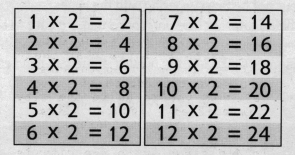

1 × 2 = 2	7 × 2 = 14
2 × 2 = 4	8 × 2 = 16
3 × 2 = 6	9 × 2 = 18
4 × 2 = 8	10 × 2 = 20
5 × 2 = 10	11 × 2 = 22
6 × 2 = 12	12 × 2 = 24

A Super Shortcut!

Multiplying a number by 2 is the same as doubling it. For example:

$$2 \times 2$$
$$= 2 + 2$$
$$= 4$$

and

$$2 \times 9$$
$$= 9 + 9$$
$$= 18$$

The Complicator has made his escape to the jungle, but not before tampering with the ropes that cross the alligator pit. The only ropes that are safe to use are those where the number at the right-hand end is the DOUBLE of the number at the left-hand end. The other ropes could send you sailing into the pit of hungry reptiles.

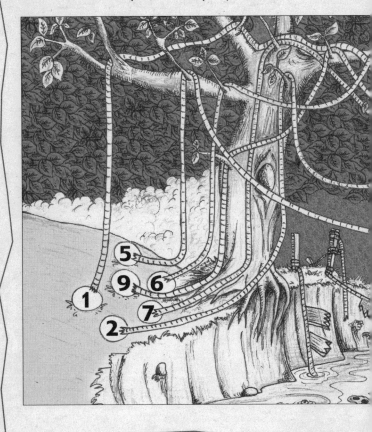

Watch out! The Complicator has also set up two booby-traps that will detonate a series of deadly bombs. You need to eliminate the two booby-traps. They are attached to the ropes that on their right-hand end have numbers that are NOT multiples of 2. Help Captain X find a safe route across the pit.

(Answers on page 86.)

Three

1 X 3 = 3	7 X 3 = 21
2 X 3 = 6	8 X 3 = 24
3 X 3 = 9	9 X 3 = 27
4 X 3 = 12	10 X 3 = 30
5 X 3 = 15	11 X 3 = 33
6 X 3 = 18	12 X 3 = 36

A Super Shortcut!

To multiply a number by 3, double it, then add it once again to the answer.

$$7 \times 3$$
$$= (7 \times 2) + 7$$
$$= 14 + 7$$
$$= 21$$

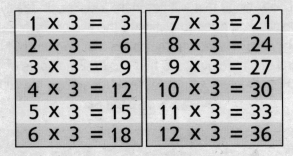

The Complicator has set up a times-table labyrinth.
At the end of each path is a sum from the 3-times
table and a possible answer. Read the sum. If you
think the answer is true, follow the path marked 'T'.
If you think the answer is false, follow 'F'. The correct
answer to each sum will point you in the right
direction and lead you through to the Complicator.

(Answers on page 87.)

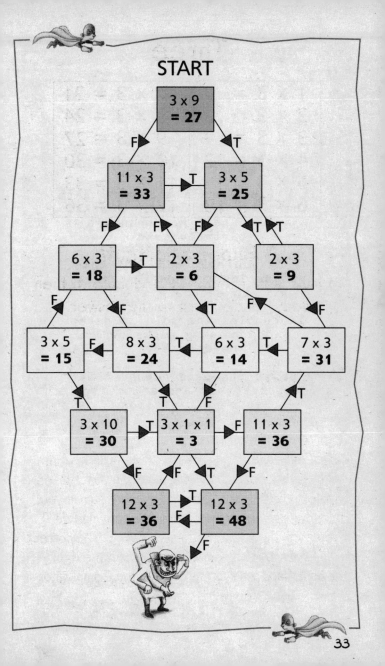

Mission 10

It's Captain X's grandma's 84th birthday and Captain X asks you to bake his granny a birthday cake.

Once you have made the cake you decide to buy 84 candles to decorate it.

If candles are sold in packs of 3, how many packs do you need to buy?

Go to the page number that matches your answer to find your next mission.

Answer on page 94.

Four

1 x 4 = 4	7 x 4 = 28
2 x 4 = 8	8 x 4 = 32
3 x 4 = 12	9 x 4 = 36
4 x 4 = 16	10 x 4 = 40
5 x 4 = 20	11 x 4 = 44
6 x 4 = 24	12 x 4 = 48

A Super Shortcut!

To multiply a number by 4, double it and then double the answer. For example:

$$3 \times 4$$
$$= 3 \times 2 \times 2$$
$$= 6 \times 2$$
$$= 12$$

You have gained entry to the Complicator's lair, but can find no trace of his secret plans. In his lab you discover a giant safe. Above the combination lock is a puzzle that reveals the code needed to open it. Work out the puzzle's missing numbers by completing the sums. Tap the numbers into the safe to discover what's inside.

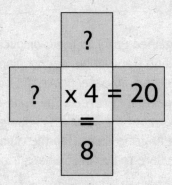

This picture shows the giant safe, and below is the
puzzle. You must work out the two missing numbers
to find the two-digit combination to the safe.

$$?$$

$$? \quad \times 4 = 20$$

$$=$$

$$8$$

But wait! The Complicator has tricked you. You have opened the safe to discover a self-destruct device. And it's ticking...

You have only a few moments to unravel the second code.
Each number in the inner circle below has been multiplied by 4 to make the number beside it in the outer circle. Can you work out the missing numbers to avoid your own self-destruction!

(Answers on page 88.)

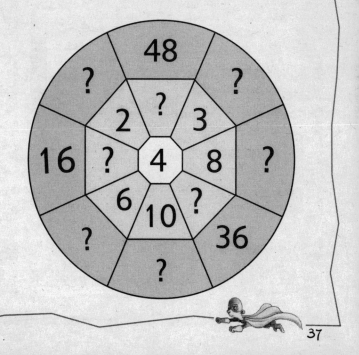

Mission 5

With all these missions you
will need a lot of energy!
So it's time to drink an
Energy Shake.
Calculate the volume of shake
each carton contains. To do
this multiply the height of
a carton by its width by its
depth. (The first one has been
done for you.)

Go to the page that matches
the highest answer for
your next mission.

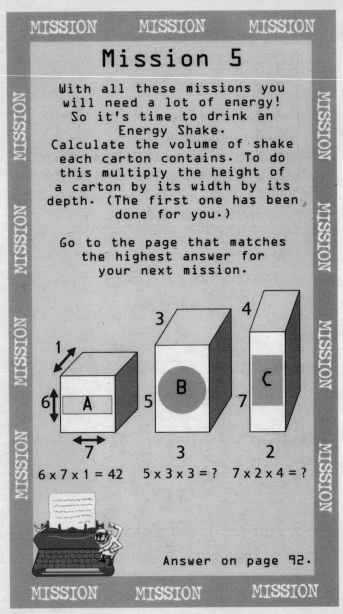

$6 \times 7 \times 1 = 42$ $5 \times 3 \times 3 = ?$ $7 \times 2 \times 4 = ?$

Answer on page 92.

Five

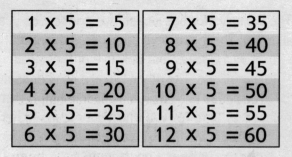

1 × 5 = 5	7 × 5 = 35
2 × 5 = 10	8 × 5 = 40
3 × 5 = 15	9 × 5 = 45
4 × 5 = 20	10 × 5 = 50
5 × 5 = 25	11 × 5 = 55
6 × 5 = 30	12 × 5 = 60

A Super Shortcut!

To multiply an even number by 5,
halve it and put 0 on the end.
For example:

$$8 \times 5$$

Half of 8 is 4. Then put 0 on the end.

$$8 \times 5 = 40$$

To multiply an odd number by 5, subtract 1,
halve that answer and put a 5 on the end.

$$7 \times 5$$

7 subtract 1 is 6, and half of 6 is 3.
Then put a 5 on the end.

$$7 \times 5 = 35$$

The Complicator has locked five princesses in a tall tower. There are seven numbered doors at the foot of the tower, but only five of them lead to a princess. The other two are dead ends. Each princess is holding a number. Multiply that number by 5 to tell you which door leads to her. Which are the five correct doors?

(Answers on page 88.)

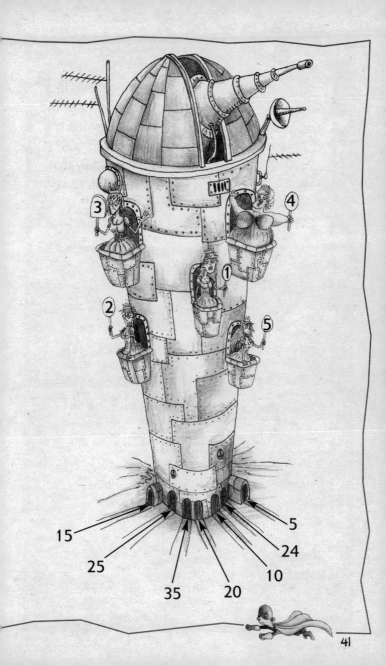

41

Mission 2

You have reached the burning
building and you can see the
people trapped inside.

There are 6 rooms, numbered
from 1 to 6. In each room
is a number of people equal
to the room number
multiplied by 3.

In total, how many people
are there to rescue?

But wait! An old lady asks you
to return to the building and
rescue her 10 budgies.

Add the 10 birds to your total
and go to this page number
for your next mission.

Answer on page 92.

Six

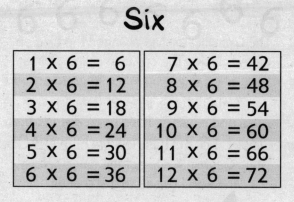

1 × 6 = 6	7 × 6 = 42
2 × 6 = 12	8 × 6 = 48
3 × 6 = 18	9 × 6 = 54
4 × 6 = 24	10 × 6 = 60
5 × 6 = 30	11 × 6 = 66
6 × 6 = 36	12 × 6 = 72

A Super Shortcut!

To multiply a number by 6, first multiply
it by 3, and then double the answer.
For example:

$$4 \times 6$$
$$= 4 \times 3 \times 2$$
$$= 12 \times 2$$
$$= 24$$

Alternatively, multiply the
number by 5, and then add it once
again to the answer.

$$7 \times 6$$
$$= (7 \times 5) + 7$$
$$= 35 + 7$$
$$= 42$$

The Complicator has changed the time on all the clocks. The city is in chaos. Nobody knows when to get up, when to go to school, or whether it's lunch or breakfast!

The hours and minutes have been divided by 6. For example, 18:30 has now become 03:05. Help Captain X correct the times before the world comes to a standstill.

To correct the clocks, multiply the hour
by **6**, then multiply the minutes by **6**.
The first clock has been corrected for you.
(Answers on page 89.)

 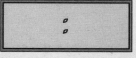

 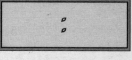

Mission 9

You walk into the Complicator's hideout, but the door closes firmly behind you and locks. It is a trap! The door is locked by a code number.

Find the code number by completing the vertical number sequences in the puzzle below. Then use the answers to complete the final horizontal pattern.

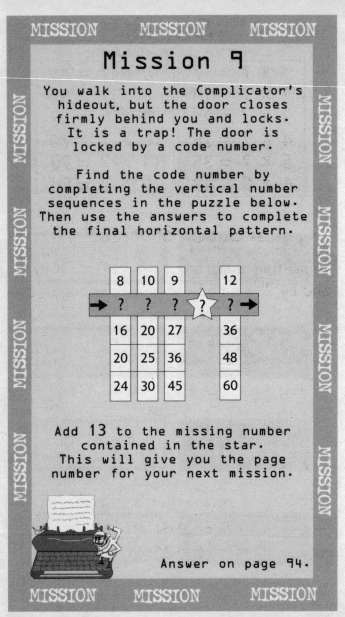

8	10	9		12		
?	?	?	?	?		
16	20	27		36		
20	25	36		48		
24	30	45		60		

Add 13 to the missing number contained in the star. This will give you the page number for your next mission.

Answer on page 94.

Seven

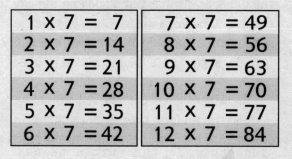

1 × 7 = 7	7 × 7 = 49
2 × 7 = 14	8 × 7 = 56
3 × 7 = 21	9 × 7 = 63
4 × 7 = 28	10 × 7 = 70
5 × 7 = 35	11 × 7 = 77
6 × 7 = 42	12 × 7 = 84

A Super Shortcut!

To multiply a number by 7, multiply it by 5
and by 2, then add the answers together.
For example:

$$7 \times 8$$
$$= (5 \times 8) + (2 \times 8)$$
$$= 40 + 16$$
$$= 56$$

and

$$7 \times 4$$
$$= (5 \times 4) + (2 \times 4)$$
$$= 20 + 8$$
$$= 28$$

The Complicator has put a spell on the city. Captain X knows a wizard who can reverse the spell using a special antidote, but he must first get the ingredients for the wizard to use.

The wizard gives Captain X a clue to help him find the towers in which the ingredients are stored. The answer to the following sums are the numbers of the towers that Captain X needs to visit.
(Answers on page 89.)

$$6 \times 7 = ?$$

$$7 \times 4 \times 2 = ?$$

$$7 \times 9 = ?$$

$$1 \times 7 \times 3 = ?$$

$$2 \times 7 \times 2 = ?$$

21 42 28 56 63 37 18

49

Now that Captain X has gathered all the ingredients, the wizard can create the antidote to the spell.

Mission 12

You have made it to the sheriff's office. A crook in jail at the office claims to know the Complicator's whereabouts. He is demanding pieces of gold for the information. The amount of gold he wants is equal to the missing number in the sequence below.

How many gold pieces is the crook asking for?

2	4	8	16	32	?

You add another 10 gold pieces and thank the crook for his help.

Go to the page number of the total amount of gold pieces you handed over to find your next mission.

Answer on page 95.

Mission 4

There are between 40 and 50 people aboard the sinking ship. The exact number of people on the ship is a square number. How many people are there?

The ship has 3 lifeboats.

If each lifeboat can carry 10 people to safety, how many people will be left on board for you to rescue?

Double this number to find the page number of your next mission.

Answer on page 92.

Eight

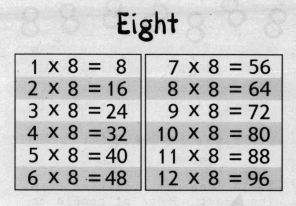

1 × 8 = 8	7 × 8 = 56
2 × 8 = 16	8 × 8 = 64
3 × 8 = 24	9 × 8 = 72
4 × 8 = 32	10 × 8 = 80
5 × 8 = 40	11 × 8 = 88
6 × 8 = 48	12 × 8 = 96

A Super Shortcut!

To multiply a number by 8, double it,
double the answer, then double
that answer. For example:

$$3 \times 8$$
$$= 3 \times 2 \times 2 \times 2$$
$$= 6 \times 2 \times 2$$
$$= 12 \times 2$$
$$= 24$$

and

$$6 \times 8$$
$$= 6 \times 2 \times 2 \times 2$$
$$= 12 \times 2 \times 2$$
$$= 24 \times 2$$
$$= 48$$

53

Captain X has decided to take a break
from saving the world, and go fishing.
However, the fish will only bite on bait that comes
from a jar labelled with a multiple of 8.

Circle the jars of bait that Captain X should use.
(Answers on page 89.)

 16
 64
 30
 10

 80 72 22

 46 56

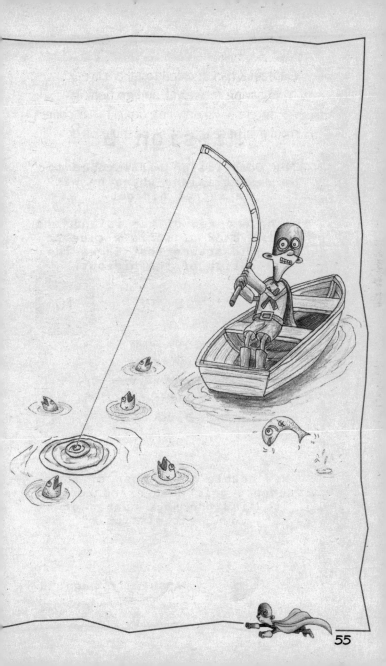

Mission 6

The Complicator has escaped to
a desert island where he has
a secret hideout.

You have a map of the island, and
on the back of it is a clue to
the grid square that marks the
location of the hideout.

Are you super
enough to see
which grid number
is a multiple of
6, of 5 and of 3?

Now double the number of the
correct grid number and add 4
to find the page number of
your next mission.

Answer on page 93.

Nine

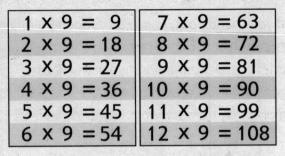

1 x 9 = 9	7 x 9 = 63
2 x 9 = 18	8 x 9 = 72
3 x 9 = 27	9 x 9 = 81
4 x 9 = 36	10 x 9 = 90
5 x 9 = 45	11 x 9 = 99
6 x 9 = 54	12 x 9 = 108

A Super Shortcut!

To multiply a number by 9,
first multiply it by 10
(find out how to do this on page 62)
and then subtract it once
from the answer. For example:

$$6 \times 9$$
$$= (6 \times 10) - 6$$
$$= 60 - 6$$
$$= 54$$

and

$$5 \times 9$$
$$= (5 \times 10) - 5$$
$$= 50 - 5$$
$$= 45$$

The X-9 Hand Trick

Hold your hands out, palms up. Choose a number (between 1 and 10). Starting at the thumb on your left hand, count along your thumb and fingers until you reach the number you want to multiply by 9, then fold that finger down.

The number of thumbs and fingers to the left of your folded finger shows the tens. The number of thumbs and fingers to the right of your folded finger shows the units. For example, if you count to 7 and fold down your seventh finger as shown below. To the left you have 6 fingers or 60 and to the right you have 3 fingers or 3, so:

$$7 \times 9 = 63$$

fold down
this finger

start here

Captain X is playing Superball. But the Complicator has sabotaged the game by turning both teams' shirts the same colour. All the players on Captain X's team have a number on their shirt that is a multiple of 9.

56

9

70

28

13

27

60

Draw a route for the ball. It must pass to each player on Captain X's team. Make sure you connect the multiples of 9 in order, from 9 to 36. Then pass the ball to Captain X so he can score the winning goal.
(Answer on page 90.)

Ten

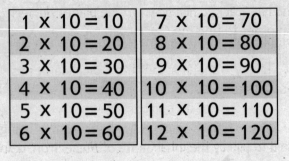

1 × 10 = 10	7 × 10 = 70
2 × 10 = 20	8 × 10 = 80
3 × 10 = 30	9 × 10 = 90
4 × 10 = 40	10 × 10 = 100
5 × 10 = 50	11 × 10 = 110
6 × 10 = 60	12 × 10 = 120

A Super Shortcut!

To multiply a number by 10, simply
put a 0 on the end of the number.
For example:

$$5 \times 10 = 50$$

$$12 \times 10 = 120$$

This super shortcut works for all numbers.

$$99 \times 10 = 990$$

$$6789 \times 10 = 67890$$

Captain X is on the trail of the Complicator
and has tracked him down to the planet Numertron.
In order to find the Complicator, Captain X must
talk to the inhabitants of Numertron using his
Trusty Translator. But the Complicator has
sabotaged Captain X's translator and multiplied
all its numbers by **10**.

Can you help Captain X translate what is being
said to him by the inhabitants of Numertron, using
your knowledge of the **10**-times table?

(Answer on page 90.)

> 190 220' 80
> 250 220 190 180 130 230
> 20 120 60!

Captain X's Trusty Translator

A = 26	H = 19	O = 12	V = 5
B = 25	I = 18	P = 11	W = 4
C = 24	J = 17	Q = 10	X = 3
D = 23	K = 16	R = 9	Y = 2
E = 22	L = 15	S = 8	Z = 1
F = 21	M = 14	T = 7	
G = 20	N = 13	U = 6	

Mission 7

You must make your way across a booby-trapped floor to deactivate a bomb. The floor is numbered like a times-table grid.
Each number in the grid is the product of the two numbers at the beginning of its row and its column. Some of the answers are incorrect, and these squares are booby-trapped to set off the bomb. You can move up or down, left or right, and diagonally. Draw the safe route across the floor to the bomb.

	5	1	3	5	4	7
3	12	1	11	30	15	21
2	9	3	6	10	8	16
8	36	8	12	24	26	38
5	25	1	21	20	18	40

Add up all the numbers in your route to reveal the page number of your next mission.

Answer on page 93.

Eleven

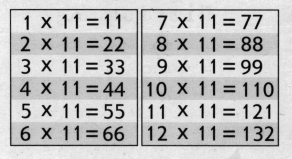

1 × 11 = 11	7 × 11 = 77
2 × 11 = 22	8 × 11 = 88
3 × 11 = 33	9 × 11 = 99
4 × 11 = 44	10 × 11 = 110
5 × 11 = 55	11 × 11 = 121
6 × 11 = 66	12 × 11 = 132

A Super Shortcut!

To multiply a one-digit number by 11,
simply write the number out twice.
For example:

$$8 \times 11 = 88$$

To multiply any two-digit number by 11,
add the two digits together, then, if the
answer is a one-digit number, put the
answer between the two digits.
For example:

$$12 \times 11$$
$$1 + 2 = \underline{3}$$
$$1 \underline{3} 2$$
$$12 \times 11 = 132$$

If the two numbers added together
make a two-digit number, you need to
do a bit of addition.

$$39 \times 11$$
$$3 + 9 = 12$$

The police have captured some of the members
of the Complicator's gang - the Crazy Elevens.
But with them is an innocent member of the public
who was passing by at the time of the raid.
All the members of the Crazy Elevens are
holding on to a card showing a multiple of 11.

What you need to do here is put the second digit in the middle and add the first digit on to the 3.

$$= \underline{4}\ \underline{2}\ 9$$
$$39 \times 11 = 429$$

Help the police identify which person
is not a member of the gang?
(Answer on page 91.)

Twelve

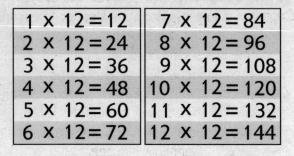

1 × 12 = 12	7 × 12 = 84
2 × 12 = 24	8 × 12 = 96
3 × 12 = 36	9 × 12 = 108
4 × 12 = 48	10 × 12 = 120
5 × 12 = 60	11 × 12 = 132
6 × 12 = 72	12 × 12 = 144

A Super Shortcut!

To multiply a number by 12, multiply it by 10 and by 2, then add the answers together. For example:

$$6 \times 12$$
$$= (6 \times 10) + (6 \times 2)$$
$$= 60 + 12$$
$$= 72$$

and

$$9 \times 12$$
$$= (9 \times 10) + (9 \times 2)$$
$$= 90 + 18$$
$$= 108$$

The Complicator has escaped into space. Captain X is looking through his super telescope and notices that someone has tampered with the stars - they've been numbered. Then suddenly he notices a pattern! Connect the multiples of 12 in order, starting from 12 and working through to 144. Finally connect back to 12, to see what Captain X can see.
(Answer on page 91.)

25
72
15
18
84
48
3
44
60
36
28
96
24
120
108
7
132
50
12
11
144
8

The '000' Rule

As you have already seen, it is very easy to multiply by 10, you simply add 0 to the end of the number.

This works for any number multiplied by 10.

$$892 \times 10$$
$$= 8920$$

This rule also works for multiplying by 100. You simply add 00 to the end.

$$892 \times 100$$
$$= 89200$$

And for 1000? You've guessed it. Simply add 000 to the end.

And what about for 10000000? Well, we'll just leave that one for you.

$$892 \times 10000000 = ?$$

BIG Numbers

Now that you have mastered the tables from
1 to 12, how about taking a look at what other,
much bigger numbers you could quickly zap in
your head?

Take a big sum like this:

$$5000 \times 70000$$

All you need to do here is work out 5×7,
which you know from the times tables and your
super shortcuts to be 35. Now count up the
zeros in the two numbers and put them all at
the end.

$$5000 \times 70000$$
$$= 350000000$$

Super Shortcuts!

To multiply a number by 99, multiply the number by 100 then subtract the original number from the answer. For example:

$$6 \times 99$$
$$= (6 \times 100) - 6$$
$$= 600 - 6$$
$$= 594$$

$$11 \times 99$$
$$= (11 \times 100) - 11$$
$$= 1100 - 11$$
$$= 1089$$

To multiply a number by 101, multiply the number by 100, then add the number to the answer. For example:

$$7 \times 101$$
$$= (7 \times 100) + 7$$
$$= 700 + 7$$
$$= 707$$

Mission 3

A ship is carrying some very important people to a meeting in the city. But the Complicator has blown a hole in the ship and it will sink in 37 minutes.

You are 6 miles away and can fly 2 miles in 4 minutes.

By the time you reach the ship, how many minutes will you have left to save the people on the ship before it sinks?

Reverse the order of the digits in your answer to find the page number of your next mission.

Answer on page 92.

Mission 13

You catch up with the Complicator
outside the bank. He's about to
run off with bags full of stolen
money. To stop him, you need
to complete the sums found on
page 76. Fill in the answers
on the money bags.

MISSION   MISSION   MISSION

MISSION

MISSION

MISSION

MISSION

MISSION

Next, you must add those answers
together to get the answer to the
long multiplication sum written
under the gun on page 77.
If you get the right answer the
Complicator will end up in jail.

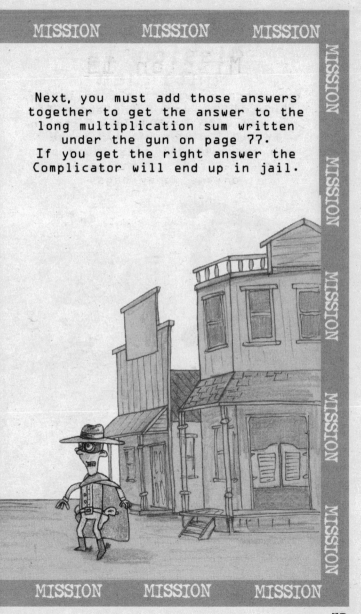

Mission 13
continued

These three sums are the stages
you need to complete the
multiplication sum 111 x 111
on page 77.

Congratulations! Your mission is complete. The Complicator is behind bars. Turn to the last page of this book for one final mission.

Your number's up Complicator!

Answers on page 95.

Mission 8

You have reached the bomb,
but you need to tap in a
code to stop it blowing up.

The code number is the prime
number missing in this series.

7 11 13 17 19 ? 29 31

Double the number of your
answer to find the page number
of your next mission.

Answer on page 93.

Units, Tens and Hundreds

So, you have mastered the times tables from
1 to 12, but could you tackle any bigger
multiplication sums the Complicator may throw
at you?

Of course you could! If you set out a sum
correctly you can use the times tables you
already know to answer any multiplication.
Take this sum:

$$4 \times 23 = ?$$

First, write out the sum putting the bigger
number on top and making sure all the units are
in the same column and all the tens are in the
same column. Like this:

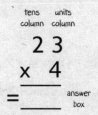

tens   units
column column

2 3
× 4
=

answer box

Split the bigger number into units and tens.
Then work out 4 multiplied by the units and
4 multiplied by the tens.

Finally add your two answers together:

```
    2 3
  x   4
  ─────
    1 2  ←——(units on bottom 4 x units on top 3)
+   8 0  ←——(units on bottom 4 x tens on top 2)
= 9 2
```

You can use this method to work out any big multiplication sum. Take this sum:

$$23 \times 41 = ?$$

Hint: You have already worked out how to do 4 x 23. As you are now multiplying by a number in the tens column, simply start by putting a 0 in the units column.

```
    2 3
  x 4 1
  ─────
    2 3  ←——(units on bottom 1 x number on top 23)
+ 9 2 0  ←——(tens on bottom 4 x number on top 23)
= 9 4 3
```

Are You Ready?

The Complicator is panicking. Are there any multiplication sums you cannot do? The world-domination plans of our villain are beginning to crumble. You have foiled the times-table crimes and followed our baddie through space and into secret lairs, rescuing innocent folk as you go. You have solved every puzzle and put the Complicator's mob of scoundrels behind bars.

But are you ready to take on the Complicator face to face and engage in a final battle of wits and strength? If the answer is yes, turn the page to begin your missions.

Begin the Missions

You are ready to begin your series
of missions. Complete the sums,
then use the answers to take you
to a page where the next problem
waits to be tackled.

The sums are in the form of word
problems. Use Captain X's
four-step trick, shown opposite, to
break down the riddle, spot the sum
and then find the answer.

A Practice Mission

You fly over the city to rescue an
old lady's cat from a tree.
Some passers-by have tried to
rescue the cat but they have all
got stuck in the tree as well!
There are 10 branches on the tree,
and 2 people stuck on each branch.

How many people have you got
to save? Then add Tiddles
the cat to your answer.

Step One. Read the problem:
try to imagine the problem.
Picture the ridiculous scene,
with all the trapped people in
the tree looking very foolish,
and Tiddles at the top with a wry
smile — pleased with the problems
he has caused.

Step Two. Sort out the
calculations: there are 10
branches multiplied by 2 people,
so the sum is 10 x 2.
Plus Tiddles, of course...

$$(10 \times 2) + 1 = ?$$

Step Three. Do the calculations:

$$10 \times 2 = 20$$
$$20 + 1 = 21$$

Step Four. Answer the problem:
look back at the question.
What is it asking?

Answer: I have 20 people to rescue
and Tiddles the cat, of course.

Now turn to page 84 for your
first mission.

MISSION   MISSION   MISSION

Mission 1

A fire has broken out in a
building at the edge of
a thick forest.

You must choose the shortest
route through the forest to
rescue the people who are
trapped in the burning building.

One route consists of 6 paths,
each 7 metres long.
The other route consists of
9 paths, each 5 metres long.

How many metres long is
the shortest route through
the forest?

The answer tells you the page
number where you will find
your next mission.

Answer on page 92.

MISSION   MISSION   MISSION

84

The Answers

Page 16

1	2	3	4	5	6	7	8	9	10	11	12
2	4	6	8	10	12	14	16	18	20	22	24
3	6	9	12	15	18	21	24	27	30	33	36
4	8	12	16	20	24	28	32	36	40	44	48
5	10	15	20	25	30	35	40	45	50	55	60
6	12	18	24	30	36	42	48	54	60	66	72
7	14	21	28	35	42	49	56	63	70	77	84
8	16	24	32	40	48	56	64	72	80	88	96
9	18	27	36	45	54	63	72	81	90	99	108
10	20	30	40	50	60	70	80	90	100	110	120
11	22	33	44	55	66	77	88	99	110	121	132
12	24	36	48	60	72	84	96	108	120	132	144

Pages 22 and 23

$9 \div 3 = 3$
$6 \div 6 = 1$
$4 \div 2 = 2$
$4 \div 4 = 1$

Page 25

The Complicator has no members in his gang because $0 \times 100 = 0$.

Page 27

$1 + 4 + 6 + 9 + 12 = 32$

So, the full address is:

32 Holdup Lane
Badville

Pages 30 and 31

Ropes 6 and 7 will get Captain X across the alligator pit safely. Ropes 11 and 13 are booby-trapped.

Page 33

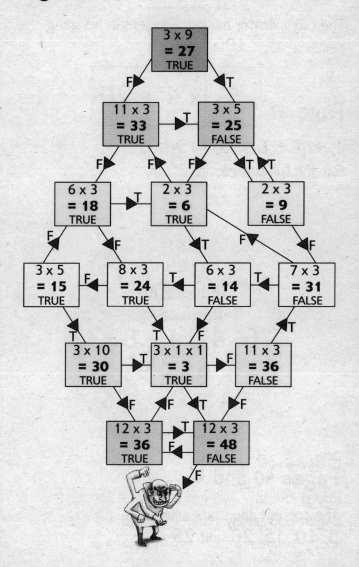

Pages 35 to 37

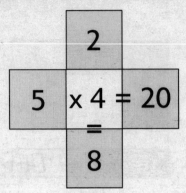

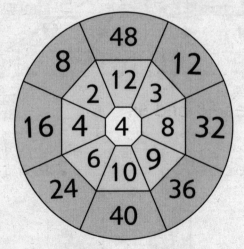

Pages 40 and 41

The correct doors are marked:
5, 10, 15, 20 and 25.

Pages 44 and 45

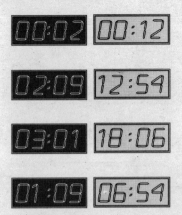

00:02	00:12
02:09	12:54
03:01	18:06
01:09	06:54

Pages 48 and 49

The towers that Captain X needs to visit are numbered 42, 56, 63, 21 and 28.

Pages 54 and 55

The jars of bait that the fish will bite on are: 16, 56, 64, 72 and 80.

Pages 60 and 61

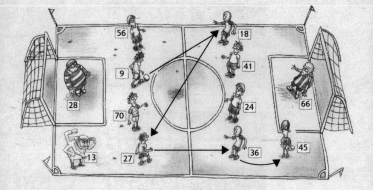

Page 63

Pages 66 and 67

Page 69

The Complicator

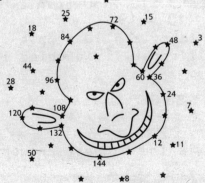

The Mission Answers

Mission 1 (page 84)
The shortest route is 42 metres long.

Mission 2 (page 42)
There are 63 people to rescue. Add 10 budgies and the total is 73.

Mission 3 (page 73)
You have 25 minutes to save the people. This number reversed is 52.

Mission 4 (page 52)
The square number is 49 (which is 7×7). The lifeboats will take $3 \times 10 = 30$ people.
$49 - 10 = 19$.
So there are 19 people without a lifeboat. 19 doubled is 38.

Mission 5 (page 38)
B: $5 \times 3 \times 3 = 45$ and
C: $7 \times 2 \times 4 = 56$
56 is the highest answer.

Mission 6 (page 56)
The hideout is in grid
number 30.
This number doubled is 60.
60 + 4 = 64

Mission 7 (page 64)

	5	1	3	5	4	7
3	12	1	11	30	15	21
2	9	3	6	10	8	16
8	36	8	12	24	26	38
5	25	1	21	20	18	40

25 + 8 + 6 + 10 + 8 + 21 = 78

Mission 8 (page 78)
The missing prime number is 23.
23 doubled is 46.

Mission 9 (page 46)

8	10	9		12
→ 12	15	18	21	24 →
16	20	27		36
20	25	36		48
24	30	45		60

$21 + 13 = 34$

Mission 10 (page 34)
$84 ÷ 3 = 28$

Mission 11 (page 28)
Flying: $7 \times 3 = 21$
X-Mobile: $(2 \times 3) + (1 \times 6) = 12$
             $12 ÷ 4 = 3$
             $3 \times 5 = 15$
The shortest time to get there
is 15 minutes.
15 reversed is 51.

Mission 12 (page 51)
The missing number in the
series is 64.
64 + 10 = 74

Mission 13 (pages 74 to 77)
111 x 100 = 11100
111 x 10 = 1110
111 x 1 = 111

$$\begin{array}{r} 111 \\ \times\,111 \\ \hline 11100 \\ 1110 \\ 111 \\ \hline = 12321 \end{array}$$

Mission 14 (page 96)

4		2		18
x		x		=
9	÷	3	=	3
=		=		x
36	÷	6	=	6

Mission 14

Now that you are able to dash from place to place, saving the world from times-table trouble, Captain X is free to catch up on some well-earned rest.
But Captain X is such a maths genius that he even dreams about maths.
Can you solve the maths problem Captain X is dreaming about?

Answers on page 95.